D1170859

ANIMAL SAFARI

Aardvarks

by Megan Borgert-Spaniol

BELLWETHER MEDIA · MINNEAPOLIS, MN

Note to Librarians, Teachers, and Parents:

Blastoff! Readers are carefully developed by literacy experts and combine standards-based content with developmentally appropriate text.

Level 1 provides the most support through repetition of high-frequency words, light text, predictable sentence patterns, and strong visual support.

Level 2 offers early readers a bit more challenge through varied simple sentences, increased text load, and less repetition of high-frequency words.

Level 3 advances early-fluent readers toward fluency through increased text and concept load, less reliance on visuals, longer sentences, and more literary language.

Level 4 builds reading stamina by providing more text per page, increased use of punctuation, greater variation in sentence patterns, and increasingly challenging vocabulary.

Level 5 encourages children to move from "learning to read" to "reading to learn" by providing even more text, varied writing styles, and less familiar topics.

Whichever book is right for your reader, Blastoff! Readers are the perfect books to build confidence and encourage a love of reading that will last a lifetime!

This edition first published in 2014 by Bellwether Media, Inc.

No part of this publication may be reproduced in whole or in part without written permission of the publisher. For information regarding permission, write to Bellwether Media, Inc., Attention: Permissions Department, 5357 Penn Avenue South, Minneapolis, MN 55419.

Library of Congress Cataloging-in-Publication Data

Borgert-Spaniol, Megan, 1989-
 Aardvarks / by Megan Borgert-Spaniol.
  p. cm. – (Blastoff! readers. Animal safari)
 Summary: "Developed by literacy experts for students in kindergarten through grade three, this book introduces aardvarks to young readers through leveled text and related photos"– Provided by publisher.
 Audience: K to grade 3.
 Includes bibliographical references and index.
 ISBN 978-1-60014-906-1 (hardcover : alk. paper)
 1. Aardvark–Juvenile literature. I. Title. II. Series: Blastoff! readers. 1, Animal safari.
 QL737.T8B67 2014
 599.3'1–dc23
                                                                    2013000879

Contents

What Are Aardvarks?

Aardvarks are **mammals** with long **snouts** and large ears.

They live in grasslands, forests, and **savannahs**.

Burrows

Aardvarks have strong legs and **claws**. They use them to dig **burrows**.

Aardvarks sleep in their burrows during the day. They stay safe and cool.

Searching for Food

Aardvarks hunt for **termites** and ants at night. They can hear and smell these **insects**.

termites

Aardvarks dig into termite mounds and anthills.

termite
mound

Their long, sticky tongues scoop up the **prey** inside.

Predators

Aardvarks keep watch for lions, hyenas, and leopards. These animals are **predators**.

Aardvarks dig holes
to escape predators.
Dig, aardvark, dig!

Glossary

burrows—holes or tunnels that some animals dig in the ground

claws—sharp, curved nails at the end of an animal's fingers and toes

insects—small animals with six legs and hard outer bodies; insect bodies are divided into three parts.

mammals—warm-blooded animals that have backbones and feed their young milk

predators—animals that hunt other animals for food

prey—animals that are hunted by other animals for food

savannahs—grasslands with scattered trees

snouts—the jaws and noses of some animals

termites—insects that feed on wood

To Learn More

AT THE LIBRARY

Brown, Marc Tolon. *Arthur Meets the President*. New York, N.Y.: LB Kids, 2008.

Gibbs, Maddie. *Aardvarks*. New York, N.Y.: PowerKids Press, 2011.

Mwalimu. *Awkward Aardvark*. London, U.K.: Hodder and Stoughton, 2005.

ON THE WEB

Learning more about aardvarks is as easy as 1, 2, 3.

1. Go to www.factsurfer.com.

2. Enter "aardvarks" into the search box.

3. Click the "Surf" button and you will see a list of related Web sites.

With factsurfer.com, finding more information is just a click away.

Index